Kjære dere tre. Det har vart for meg
ei stor glede å ha dere på denne
turen. Det er også alltid moro å ha
barn med så, takk for at dere tok
Evan med dere.

Kjærlig hilsen
Mari Anne (Roppe)
13834 EAST DIAMOND ROAD
GILBERT, AZ 85297
maroppe @ cox. net

THE
QUIET ROOM

*...is an infinite landscape, one in which you are free to roam,
rest and sit awhile to enjoy the solitude. In the quiet room it is your senses that guide you.
Its sights, sounds and scents allure you, delight you, stir something deep in you.
Listen, look - and enjoy all it offers.*

The days keep coming, coming--
They watch me,
waiting,
full of expectant light.

Hans Børli (trans. E. Fraser)

Trysil

It seemed as if the hour were one
Sent from beyond the skies,
Which scattered from above the sun
A light of Paradise.

P.B. Shelley

Råde, Østfold

Now fades the glimmering landscape on the sight,
And all the air a solemn stillness holds.

Thomas Gray

Jøsenfjorden

...between us and the sky, there lies but silence; and there in the stillness let us listen to the voice that is speaking within us.

Jerome K. Jerome

Kjerag, Lysefjorden

I come into the presence of still water.
And I feel above me the day-blind stars
waiting with their light.

Wendell Berry

And the day climbs down from its blue loft-bed
on a slanting ladder of sunbeams,
pauses a moment between the trees,
airy-light, young.

Hans Børli (trans. E. Fraser)

Listen in the east and listen in the west, but listen!
That is the everlasting God! This stillness, murmuring in my ear
is the blood of all nature seething, is God weaving through the world and through me.

Knut Hamsun (trans. James W. McFarlane)

Holmevann, Åmli

Silently homewards
with my modest catch.
Fish dart brightly in the depths.
The oars move softly
in rowlocks wet with morning.

Tarjei Vesaas (trans. E. Fraser / O. Grinde)

Methinks, it should have been impossible
Not to love all things in a world so filled;
Where the breeze warbles, and the mute still air
Is Music slumbering on her instrument.

S.T. Coleridge

Aurlandsfjorden

Listen! You hear the grating roar
Of pebbles which the waves draw back, and fling,
At their return, up the high strand,
Begin, and cease, and then again begin
With tremulous cadence slow, and bring
The eternal note of sadness in.

Matthew Arnold

Børaunen, Randaberg

Sunset in the ethereal waves:
I cannot tell if the day
is ending, or the world, or if
the secret of secrets is inside me again.

Anna Akhmatova (trans. Jane Kenyon)

Come to me in the silence of the night;
Come in the speaking silence of a dream.

Christina Rossetti

Midnightsun at Flakstad, Lofoten

Sweet the coming on
Of grateful evening mild, then silent night
With this her solemn bird and this fair moon,
And these the gems of heaven, her starry train.

John Milton

It is that dream we carry
that something miraculous will happen
that it must happen -

that time will open
that the heart will open
that doors will open
and that the rockface will open
that springs will gush forth -

that the dream will open
and that one morning we'll glide in
to a harbour we didn't know was there.

Olav H. Hauge (trans. O. Grinde)

Sssh says the ocean
Sssh says the small wave at the shore - sssh
not so violent, not
so proud, not
so remarkable.

Feistein Fyr, Jæren

Sssh
says the surf
crowding around the outcrops,
washing the shore. Sssh,

they say to people,
this is _our_ Earth,
our eternity.

Rolf Jacobsen (trans. O. Grinde)

-- these steep and lofty cliffs,
That on a wild and secluded scene impress
Thoughts of more deep seclusion; and connect
The landscape with the quiet of the sky.

W. Wordsworth

We don't know God's heart,
but we know
something that pours out over us
like rain over our hands.

We don't see His eyes,
but we see
invisible light over everything
as on a summer night.

We don't hear His voice,
but we find
roads everywhere and signs in our hearts
and paths with hushed light.

Rolf Jacobsen (trans. O. Grinde)

Full many a glorious morning have I seen
Flatter the mountain tops with sovereign eye,
Kissing with golden face the meadows green,
Gilding pale streams with heavenly alchemy

W. Shakespeare

Østmarka, Oslo

The clouds roll on.
Silent as sleepwalkers the clouds
keep coming from infinity

Døråldalen, Rondane

bank behind bank
and line after line,
and change colors on the earth.

Rolf Jacobsen (trans. by R. Greenwald)

Sea-birds are asleep,
The world forgets to weep,
Sea murmurs her sweet slumber-song
On the shadowy sand
Of this elfen land.

from Elgar's Sea Pictures

Hå på Jæren

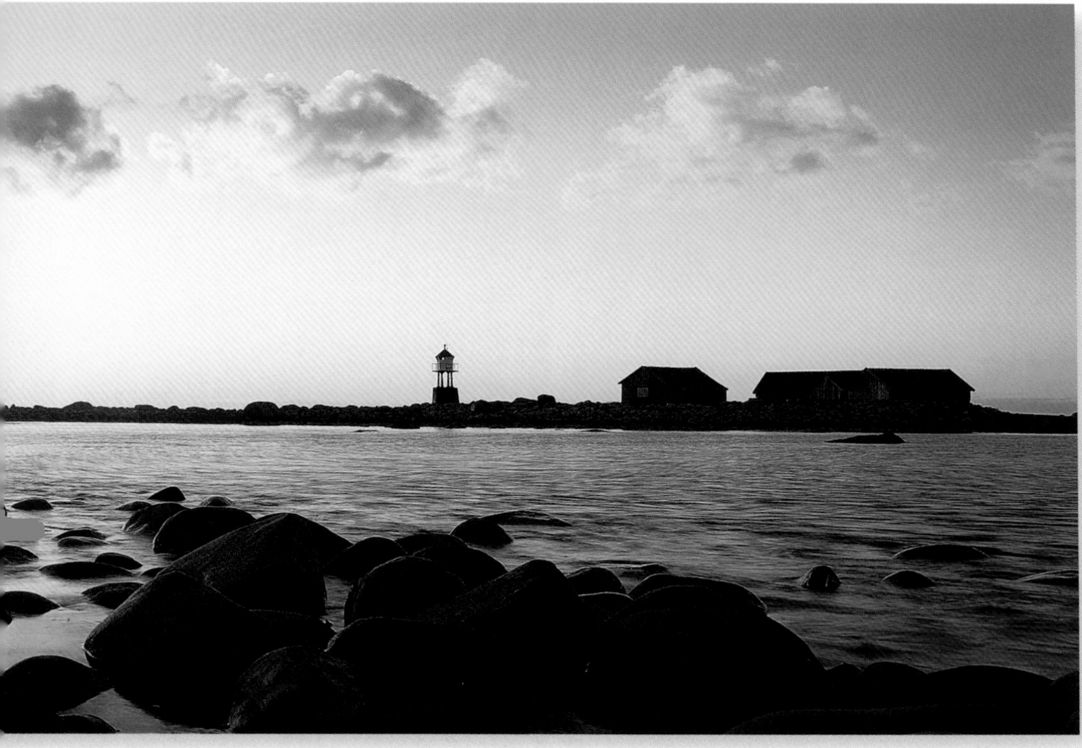

If you go far enough out
you can see the Universe itself,
all the billion light years summed up time
only as a flash, just as lonely, as distant as a star on a June night
if you go far enough out.

Rondane

And still, my friend, if you go far enough out
you are only at the beginning

- of yourself.

Rolf Jacobsen (trans. Olav Grinde)

It is people at the edge who say
Things at the edge: winter is towards knowing.

William Stafford

Was it light?
Was it light within?
Was it light within light?
Stillness becoming alive,
Yet still?

Theodore Roethke

Otta, Oppland

WE CAN ALSO RECOMMEND THE BOOK "PANORAMA NORGE"

Editor: Jens-Uwe Kumpch
Texts chosen by E. Fraser and J.U. Kumpch
Idea and lay-out: Natur og Kulturforlaget A.S

Hans Børli: "Dagene" (Days), (excerpt), trans. by E. Fraser from Dagene, Aschehoug/Oslo 1958

Wendell Berry: "The Peace of Wild Things", (excerpt), from Openings, Harcourt Brace Jovanovic, 1968

Hans Børli: "Sommermorgen i skogen" (excerpt) (Summer morning in the forest), (excerpt), from Hver liten ting, trans. by E. Fraser Aschehoug/Oslo 1964

Knut Hamsun: Excerpt from Pan, Alkin Books Ltd., Windmill Grove 1994

Tarjei Vesaas: "Morgon på Vinjevatnet" (excerpt) (Morning at the Lake Vinjevatn), (excerpt), trans. by Olav Grinde, from Liv ved straumen, Gyldendal Norsk Forlag/Oslo 1970

Akhmatova poem translated by Jane Kenyon, quoted in: Robert Bly (ed.); News of the Universe, Harper & Row Publ. Inc. 1980

Olav H. Hauge: "It's that dream", trans. by Olav Grinde, from: Dikt i samling (Collected poems), Det Norske Samlaget/Oslo 1994

Rolf Jacobsen: "Breathing Exercise" (excerpt) from: Night Open - selected poems of Rolf Jacobsen, trans. by Olav Grinde, White Pine Press, Buffalo, New York 1993

Rolf Jacobsen: "The Clouds" (excerpt), in The Silence Afterwards: Selected Poems of Rolf Jacobsen, trans. and ed. by Roger Greenwald (Princeton Univ. Press, 1985)

William Stafford: "Sayings from the Northern Ice" (excerpt), quoted in: Robert Bly; News of the Universe, Harper & Row Publ. Inc. 1980

Theodore Roethke: "The Lost Son" (excerpt), from Praise to the End, Faber & Faber Ltd. 1948/51

Photographers: Trysil, Jørn Arelett Omre/NN/Samfoto -Råde, Østfold, Pål Hermansen/NN/Samfoto -Jøsenfjorden, Snorre Aske -Kjerag i Lysefjorden, Snorre Aske -Skogstjern, Snorre Aske -Motlys, Snorre Aske-Holmevann i Åmli, Snorre Aske -Jølstervatnet, Snorre Aske -Aurlandsfjorden, Snorre Aske -Børaunen, Randaberg, Snorre Aske -Nordsjøen, Snorre Aske -Flakstad i Lofoten, Pål Hermansen/NN/Samfoto -Rendalen, Steinar Myhr/NN/Samfoto -Kjerringøy, Per Eide/Samfoto -Feistein Fyr på Jæren, Snorre Aske -Preikestolen i Lysefjorden, Snorre Aske -Omastrand i Hardanger, Snorre Aske -Østmarka ved Oslo, Pål Hermansen/NN/Samfoto -Døråldalen, Rondane, Pål Hermansen/NN/Samfoto -Hå på Jæren, Snorre Aske - Rondane, J.B. Olsen/R. Sørensen/NN/Samfoto -Kvalsundet i Troms, Pål Hermansen/NN/Samfoto -Otta i Oppland, Bård Løken NN/Samfoto